# SNOOPY

( features as )

# The Sportsman

**Charles M. Schulz**

ЯR

PEANUTS is a registered trademark of United Feature Syndicate, Inc.
Based on the PEANUTS® comic strip by Charles M. Schulz.

Originally published in 1988 as 'Snoopy Stars as the Sportsman'.
This edition published in the Year 2001 by Ravette Publishing.

Printed and bound in Great Britain
for Ravette Publishing Limited,
Unit 3, Tristar Centre,
Star Road, Partridge Green,
West Sussex  RH13 8RA
by Cox & Wyman, Berkshire

ISBN: 1 84161 105 0

TO GILLIAN,

HAPPY BIRTHDAY 2002.

♡Kevin x, Jane x xo

Peter
x

5-14 © 1988 United Feature Syndicate, Inc.

**PEANUTS**

9-11   Tm Reg U.S Pat. Off · All rights reserved
© 1971 by United Feature Syndicate, Inc

SCHULZ

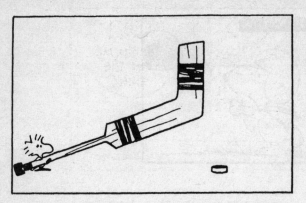

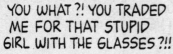

© 1988 United Feature Syndicate, Inc.    3-7

SORRY I MISSED THAT ONE, MANAGER...MAYBE MY GLOVE ISN'T BIG ENOUGH...

BIG ENOUGH?! HA! YOU KNOW WHAT YOU NEED?

© 1988 United Feature Syndicate, Inc.

3-11

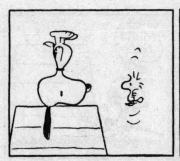

5-5

WOODSTOCK IS REALLY INTO HOPSCOTCH

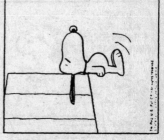

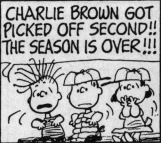

PEANUTS

I HAVE A "TRIVIA" SPORTS QUESTION THAT WILL DRIVE WOODSTOCK UP THE WALL!

2-21

"WHO PLAYED SHORTSTOP FOR ST. PAUL WHEN THEY WON THE AMERICAN ASSOCIATION PENNANT IN NINETEEN THIRTY-EIGHT?"

HOW'D HE EVER HEAR OF OLLIE BEJMA?

SCHULZ

© 1977 United Feature Syndicate, Inc.

6-1

LET'S TRY SOMETHING DIFFERENT FOR THE KICKOFF...

INSTEAD OF HAVING SOMEONE HOLD THE BALL WITH HIS FINGER, LET'S USE A KICKING TEE...

11-8

A KICKING TEE...RIGHT!

© 1978 United Feature Syndicate, Inc.

SCHULZ

EVERYBODY CAN GO HOME! IT LOOKS LIKE IT ISN'T GOING TO STOP RAINING...EVERYBODY CAN GO HOME!

© 1980 United Feature Syndicate, Inc.

IT'S HARD TO TELL EVERYBODY TO GO HOME WHEN NO ONE SHOWED UP!

© 1981 United Feature Syndicate, Inc.

8-4

THAT'S THE RULE...IF THE BALL ROLLS OVER YOU, YOU GET TO GO TO FIRST BASE...

SCHULZ

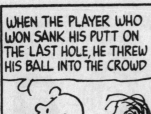

IT'S A JUNIOR BOWLING TOURNAMENT...I WONDER IF I SHOULD ENTER...

YOU'D JUST LOSE

THAT'S ALL RIGHT.. THERE'S TOO MUCH EMPHASIS THESE DAYS ON WINNING

10-20

SOMETIMES I WONDER IF SOME ATHLETES EVEN ENJOY PLAYING...

© 1982 United Feature Syndicate, Inc.

THAT'S WHAT I'D LIKE TO BE..SOMEONE WHO DOESN'T ENJOY PLAYING, BUT WINS ALL THE TIME!

**Other PEANUTS titles published by Ravette ...**

**Snoopy Pocket Books**

| *Snoopy features as ...* | **ISBN** | **Price** |
|---|---|---|
| Man's Best Friend | 1 84161 066 6 | £2.99 |
| Master of the Fairways | 1 84161 067 4 | £2.99 |
| The Fearless Leader | 1 84161 104 2 | £2.99 |
| The Fitness Fanatic | 1 84161 029 1 | £2.99 |
| The Flying Ace | 1 84161 027 5 | £2.99 |
| The Great Philosopher | 1 84161 064 X | £2.99 |
| The Legal Beagle | 1 84161 065 8 | £2.99 |
| The Literary Ace | 1 84161 026 7 | £2.99 |
| The Master Chef | 1 84161 107 7 | £2.99 |
| The Matchmaker | 1 84161 028 3 | £2.99 |
| The Music Lover | 1 84161 106 9 | £2.99 |

**Peanuts 'Little Book' series**

| | | |
|---|---|---|
| Charlie Brown - Wisdom | 1 84161 099 2 | £2.50 |
| Snoopy - Laughter | 1 84161 100 X | £2.50 |
| Lucy - Advice | 1 84161 101 8 | £2.50 |
| Peppermint Patty - Blunders | 1 84161 102 6 | £2.50 |

| | | |
|---|---|---|
| Peanuts Anniversary Treasury | 1 84161 021 6 | £9.99 |
| Peanuts Treasury | 1 84161 043 7 | £9.99 |

| | | |
|---|---|---|
| You Really Don't Look 50 Charlie Brown | 1 84161 020 8 | £7.99 |

**Snoopy's Laughter and Learning series**
*wipe clean pages*
(a fun series of story and activity books for preschool
 and infant school children)

| | | |
|---|---|---|
| Book 1 - Read With Snoopy | 1 84161 016 X | £2.50 |
| Book 2 - Write With Snoopy | 1 84161 017 8 | £2.50 |
| Book 3 - Count With Snoopy | 1 84161 018 6 | £2.50 |
| Book 4 - Colour With Snoopy | 1 84161 019 4 | £2.50 |

All PEANUTS™ books are available from your local bookshop or
from the address below. Just tick the titles required and send the
form with your payment to:-

BBCS, P.O. Box 941, Kingston upon Hull HU1 3YQ
24-hr telephone credit card line 01482 224626

Prices and availability are subject to change without prior notice.

Please enclose a cheque or postal order made payable to BBCS to
the value of the cover price of the book and allow the following for
postage and packing:-

| UK & BFPO: | £1.95 (weight up to 1kg) | 3-day delivery |
| | £2.95 (weight over 1kg up to 20kg) | 3-day delivery |
| | £4.95 (weight up to 20kg) | next day delivery |

| EU & Eire: | Surface Mail: | £2.50 for first book & £1.50 for subsequent books |
| | Airmail: | £4.00 for first book & £2.50 for subsequent books |

| USA: | Surface Mail: | £4.50 for first book & £2.50 for subsequent books |
| | Airmail: | £7.50 for first book & £3.50 for subsequent books |

| Rest of | Surface Mail: | £6.00 for first book & £3.50 for subsequent books |
| the World: | Airmail: | £10.00 for first book & £4.50 for subsequent books |

Name: ...................................................................................

Address: ...................................................................................

...................................................................................

...................................................................................

Cards accepted: Visa, Mastercard, Switch, Delta, American Express

| | | | | | | | | | | | | | | | | | | |
|--|--|--|--|--|--|--|--|--|--|--|--|--|--|--|--|--|--|--|

Expiry date ..................................... Signature ...................................................